Go Confident

A Teen Boy's Guide to Overcoming Fear and Anxiety

OPEYEMI ADEBAYO

Go Confident

Copyright ©2025 by Opeyemi Adebayo

Paperback ISBN: 978-1-965593-60-8

All rights reserved. No part of this publication may be reproduced, distributed, or transmitted in any form or by any means, including photocopying, recording, or other electronic or mechanical methods without the prior written permission of the author except in the case of brief quotations embodied in reviews and certain other non-commercial uses permitted by copyright law.

Published by Cornerstone Publishing

A Division of Cornerstone Creativity Group LLC
Info@thecornerstonepublishers.com
www.thecornerstonepublishers.com

Author's Contact

To book the author to speak at your next event or to order bulk copies of this book, please, use the information below:
Opeoadebayo@gmail.com

Printed in the United States of America.

DEDICATION

I dedicate this book, *Go Confident*, to the Almighty God, whose grace, guidance, and unwavering faithfulness have made this journey possible. To You be all the glory, honor, and adoration. Thank You, Lord.

I also dedicate this book to all the amazing teen boys out there. May you be empowered, inspired, and reminded of your God-given potential as you go confidently into the world.

FOREWORD

I am deeply honored and privileged to write the foreword to this exceptional book on an ever relevant and critical subject: **Confidence**. Confidence is as vital in the boardroom as it is in the bedroom, as indispensable in warfare as it is in our welfare. It permeates every aspect of our daily lives and decisions.

Having known Dr. (Mrs.) Opeyemi Adebayo for several years, I can confidently say she is uniquely qualified to write this book. As someone who has navigated profound challenges and undertaken diverse tasks from academia to spiritual leadership, Dr. Opeyemi is a certified coach, speaker, entrepreneur, and an indefatigable trailblazer. Her insights on this subject are not only profound but also highly practical.

This book explores confidence in a way that resonates with teens and adults alike. Teenagers will find encouragement and enlightenment within its pages, while parents, teachers, and guardians will discover a helpful guide to instruct and support the younger generation. Dr. Opeyemi skillfully delves into self-worth, self-esteem, and self-awareness, uncovering the causes of low confidence and offering actionable strategies to build confidence and sustain it.

The section titled "What Confidence Is Not" is particularly powerful. Phrases such as "Confidence doesn't have to be loud" offer liberation for introverts often misjudged as lacking confidence. This aligns beautifully with Isaiah 30:15b KJV: *"In quietness and in confidence shall be your strength."*. The section on why teenagers struggle with confidence is equally compelling, exposing root causes and providing practical steps for overcoming these challenges. Dr. Opeyemi's balanced discussion of nature versus nurture illustrates how both genetic makeup and environmental influences including spiritual growth shape confidence.

The book culminates with a challenge for competence, highlighting that confidence without substance is folly. In the closing chapter, Dr. Opeyemi emphasizes the importance of preparation, practice, and skill development as the foundation of genuine confidence. This serves as a timely reminder for teens to diligently hone their God-given talents and skills. 1 Chronicles 12:8 *"And of the Gadites there separated themselves unto David into the hold to the wilderness men of might, and men of war fit for the battle, that could handle shield and buckler, whose faces were like the faces of lions, and were as swift as the roes upon the mountains;"* describing men of war who were swift, skilled, and confident warriors is an apt illustration of what our children can aspire to be: individuals who walk confidently through life, fulfilling their God-given purpose.

With its seamless integration of scripture, practical advice, and life-tested principles, this book is a roadmap for building confidence a critical life skill that will serve young people in their present and future endeavors. I encourage you to read it thoughtfully, meditate on its lessons, and draw strength from its wisdom.

Finally, don't miss Dr. Opeyemi Adebayo's other inspiring books, *Greatness in You* and *The Shift*, which are sure to motivate you to discover your God-given potential, embrace your true self, and live out your divine purpose.

Adedayo Adeogba

CONTENTS

Dedication Iii
Foreword Iv
Acknowledgments Viii
Your Guide To Unshakable Confidence Xi

1. Discover Self Confidence 1
2. The Power Of Confidence..................................... 13
3. Know Who You Are 25
4. Strive For Competence In Everything You Do 37
5. Embrace A Growth Mindset 51
6. Self-Confidence Habits 67
7. Develop God Confidence 79
8. Live The Fearless Life 89
9. Mentorship And Confidence: The Role Of Role Models 101

Daily Prayer For Teen Boy 107

ACKNOWLEDGMENTS

I wish to express my sincere gratitude to the remarkable individuals who have made this journey possible.

First and foremost, I am profoundly grateful to Deacon Adedayo Adeogba for his invaluable contribution to this book. His heartfelt foreword, unwavering prayers, and steadfast support have been a source of inspiration and encouragement throughout this journey. I deeply appreciate his wisdom, guidance, and the time he dedicated to bringing this project to life.

I extend my gratitude to Pastor Gbenga Showunmi and the team at Cornerstone Publishing for their meticulous attention to detail and dedication in preparing this manuscript, ensuring the successful completion of this project.

To my beloved family, my husband, Raphael, and my son, David, thank you for your unwavering support, love, and encouragement. Your presence and prayers have been a constant source of motivation throughout this journey. I love you both.

I also wish to acknowledge my extended family and friends whose timely support, encouragement, and prayers contributed to bringing this vision to life. Your generosity and faith in this project are sincerely appreciated.

Introduction
YOUR GUIDE TO UNSHAKABLE CONFIDENCE

Let's face it: being a teenage boy is not always easy. Every day, you face challenges and try hard to figure out how to live. You're expected to navigate school life, excel academically, deal with changes in your body, and maintain a healthy online and offline social presence. You may also need to plan for college, manage family expectations, deal with friendships, and figure out who you are. And you are supposed to feel confident in the midst of all that!

Are you the guy who rehearses the answer three times in your head before raising your hand in class, only to keep it down anyway? Perhaps you have incredible ideas for the school project or the next big app but keep them locked away because you're unsure how others might react. Or maybe you're the talented athlete who holds back from showing your full potential because you're afraid of making mistakes in front of everyone. This book is definitely for you if you are a teenage boy dealing with such struggles.

Imagine walking into a room and feeling completely at ease, knowing who you are and what you're capable of. Picture yourself raising your hand in class without that knot in your stomach or stepping up to take that game-winning shot without second-guessing yourself. Think about confidently pursuing your dreams without letting that nagging voice of self-doubt hold you back. That is what confidence is all about.

This book is your practical guide to building unshakeable confidence. I'm talking about the kind of confidence that sticks with you, even when things get hard, or you're hit with surprises. Think of this book as your guide to becoming the strong, confident, and capable young man you're meant to be.

We will not assume that building self-confidence is as simple as repeating positive affirmations in the mirror (though that can help). Instead, we will dig deep into the actual techniques of confidence, understanding what truly makes someone confident, and showing you how you can intentionally build yours.

I want you to understand that confidence is not something you are born with but a skill you can learn and improve upon, just like you can get better at a video game or master a new sport. And that's exactly what we're going to do in this book. It will introduce you to several "hacks" that will help you:

- Understand who you are and embrace your unique qualities
- Conquer fear and self-doubt so you can step up and take action
- Build skills that make you feel capable and strong
- Handle setbacks with resilience, staying calm and focused
- Stand up confidently for yourself and support others
- Unlock your God-confidence
- Build habits that boost your self-confidence

This book is a practical guide to help you build unshakable confidence, no matter the circumstances. By reading it, you'll gain the tools, mindset, and strategies necessary to tackle any challenge that comes your way with assurance and poise. Whether it's stepping up for an exam, presenting in front of a group, speaking the truth in conversations, or simply gaining self-assurance in everyday situations, this book provides you with the step-by-step approach to unlocking your inner confidence. It's time to stop second-guessing yourself and start embracing your true potential because confidence is a skill that can be developed, and by the end of this book, you'll know exactly how to master it!

DISCOVER SELF CONFIDENCE

CHAPTER ONE
DISCOVER SELF CONFIDENCE

If you have confidence, you have one most important requirements for your success.

Confidence is a superpower essential for getting ahead in life. If you are looking for one trait that will position you on a path to exceptional success in life, go for confidence. We live in a world filled with challenges that can undermine our efforts. If you are going to excel, you must learn to stand up for yourself and develop the confidence that empowers you to face life head-on. Without a certain level of confidence, life will not only be difficult, but it can also feel nearly impossible. You cannot navigate the difficulties and resistance of life without the confidence needed to face and overcome them.

Self-confidence is a powerful requirement for academic success, relationships, and life as a whole. And when it comes to teenage boys, it becomes even more important. As a teenage boy, you're at a crucial point in your life where you must develop yourself for the future. The confidence you build now will be the foundation for your future success. It will help you navigate the challenges of high school, make meaningful friends, pursue your passions, and eventually excel in your career and relationships. That is not to say you cannot build your confidence later in life, but I suggest you start cultivating it now.

Let's define confidence

What exactly is self-confidence? What do we mean when we say that someone is self-confident? We are going to break it down so you can understand it better. But before we go deeper into the definitions of self-confidence, we will look at three other related terms briefly: self-worth, self-esteem, and self-awareness.

1. Self-Worth

It is the belief that you are valuable, regardless of what you do or achieve. Self-worth is about loving yourself unconditionally.

2. Self-Esteem

Self-esteem is how you feel about yourself overall. It includes your sense of self-worth and confidence in different areas of life.

3. Self-Awareness:

Self-awareness is like having a map of yourself. Knowing who you are and what you stand for makes it easier to feel confident in your decisions and actions. Self-awareness helps you set goals that matter to you and gives you the courage to pursue them. In a later chapter, we will discuss this in more detail and see how it impacts your confidence.

SELF-CONFIDENCE AT A GLANCE

Self-confidence is about believing in yourself and your abilities enough to take necessary action. It is the inner voice that reassures you when you face a challenge. Here is a definition I love: self-confidence is the willingness to try something out no matter how you feel. Self-confidence isn't a feeling; it's the courage to try new things, even when you're not sure how they'll turn out.

You may say, "What if it doesn't work?" And my response to you is, what if it works? In the end, it is always better to try than to cry. And if you don't try, how will you know what works and what doesn't? By stepping out confidently, you discover a path to your success.

When you believe in your ability to handle specific situations or tasks, you are confident. Self-confidence is the willingness to step up, take risks, and go after what you want, even when you're not 100% sure of the outcome. It's about believing in your ability to learn, grow, and overcome challenges. We may not plan for these challenges, but whenever they show up, you know within yourself that you are capable of handling them, no matter their size or shape. As Philippians 4:13 reminds us, I can do all things through Christ who strengthens me.

WHAT CONFIDENCE IS NOT?

1. Confidence Is Not A Feeling But An Act.

Many young people struggle with being confident because they relate self-confidence to their feelings instead of their actions. It is founded on an inner certainty that comes from the deep ends of your worth, ability, and experience. When you are genuinely sure that something will work out for the better, you are more likely to take action. That action will produce excellent results, and those results will further reinforce your certainty to take more action, and the cycle goes on and on. I'm pretty sure you understand. The belief that you are worthwhile and capable makes you enthusiastic, and that comes when you are certain of your abilities and act courageously to face challenges. In the end, confidence turns thought into action.

2. Confidence Is Not The Absence Of Fear.

Being confident doesn't mean you are never afraid or unsure of yourself. Many times, confident people are uncertain about what they are going to do. The difference is that they don't let these fears stop them. They take action despite their fear and anxiety.

3. Confidence Is Not About Loudness.

Quiet confidence is just as powerful. It's about being comfortable with who you are, not about being the loudest in the room. You can be loud and still lack confidence; sometimes, that noise is simply a way to mask insecurities.

4. Confidence Does Not Mean Everyday Success.

Confident people don't necessarily succeed all the time. Sometimes, they miss the mark too. But they are always willing to try. They're not afraid to fail because they understand that failure is an opportunity to learn, unlearn, relearn, and grow from their mistakes.

KEY REASONS WHY YOUNG PEOPLE LACK CONFIDENCE

Many young people struggle with confidence and standing up when it matters. It's important to understand this because it will help you overcome these challenges. While the factors listed below are common among young people, they are not permanent. Let's look at a few of them:

1. **Comparison Trap:**

Comparing yourself with others is unhealthy. When you make it a habit, you place yourself under unnecessary pressure, making you feel inadequate based on who you are comparing yourself with. And in this era of social media, you have to be careful, as it makes it easy to compare yourself to others, which can lead to feelings of inadequacy. Often, what you see about others that cause this pressure isn't real but carefully crafted make-believe.

2. **Fear of Failure:**

Many young people are afraid of trying new things because they fear failure or worry about looking foolish. But it's important to understand that failure is a vital part of growth. Failure and success are two sides of the same coin. The more you try, the more you may fail, and ultimately, the more you will succeed. So, you have to be willing to try new things.

3. Negative Self-Talk:

Nothing undermines your confidence like negative self-talk. Your self-talk is that little voice in your head that says you can't do something or reminds you of how complex or risky a situation can be. This can be very damaging if you don't control it.

4. Lack Of Experience:

Experience is one of the best ways to build self-confidence. When you do something repeatedly, you develop what's known as conscious competence. That means you know you can do it, which makes you more confident in that particular task. But when you lack experience, even with simple tasks, you may hesitate to try, feeling unsure of your abilities.

5. Body Image Issues:

Going through puberty and dealing with body changes can make you feel insecure. As your body chemistry changes, it can lead to feelings of discomfort or low-selfesteem, which can affect your confidence. However, with knowledge, you can take charge of your body and do what's necessary to express your confidence.

6. Academic Pressure:

The stress of achieving good grades and planning for the future can sometimes shake your confidence. That is why you need mentors and role models who have been through that phase of life and have the experience to help you cope with such pressures.

YOU CAN CULTIVATE IT

One of the most powerful things about confidence is that it is a skill. It is not something you are born with but a skill that anyone can develop. It is something you can both learn and improve upon over time.

A lot of young people assume that confidence is just a personality trait. They believe you are either born with it or can't be confident. Others think it is for the "cool kids" or naturally outgoing individuals. Well, that's not true at all! Confidence is like a muscle; the more you practice it, the stronger it becomes.

I want you to see it as something akin to learning to play a particular sport or musical instrument. At first, you might feel unsure, but with consistent practice, you improve and become more confident.

You can build your confidence through training and by challenging yourself to do new and difficult tasks. Every time you step out to do something new despite your fear, you're building that confidence muscle.

When you discover self-confidence and understand that you can intentionally cultivate it, you no longer have to hold back. Every confident person you admire started where you are now. Remember that they were NOT necessarily born with it, but through consistency, determination, and practice, they were able to cultivate it over time, one step at a time. And I want you to know that if they can, so can you.

When you realize that self-confidence can be intentionally developed, you no longer have to hold back. Every confident person you admire started where you are now. Remember, they weren't necessarily born with confidence; through consistency, determination, and practice, they built it over time, one step at a time. And if they could do it, so can you.

THE POWER OF CONFIDENCE

2

CHAPTER TWO
THE POWER OF CONFIDENCE

"Confidence matters to everyone and in every aspect of life".

Confidence is the secret ingredient that can take you from "average" to "excellence" in every area of your life. Think of it as the fuel that powers your dreams and ambitions. No matter how fantastic or fast a car may be, it will never move an inch if you don't fill it with gas. In other words, you may know where you are headed in life, but you won't get there if you lack confidence. So, does confidence matter? you may ask. Well, it does, and that is what this chapter is all about.

Confidence matters in every area of your life, from school to relationships to future success. Many people fail to realize that life rewards only those who are confident in who they are and what they can do. When you know who you are and what you can do, you will believe in yourself. That belief will empower you to speak up when necessary. By speaking up and putting yourself out there, you unlock powerful opportunities for yourself.

When you are confident, not only can you project yourself for opportunities, but you can also project your ideas. By sharing your ideas, you gain the support of people who will help you achieve your dreams. Self-confidence will position you to stand tall against life's challenges and succeed where others fail.

Embrace your confidence.

On the other hand, a lack of self-confidence can make you vulnerable to failure. When you lack confidence, you are likely to miss many powerful opportunities. Worse, a lack of self-confidence can undermine your talents. No matter how skilled you are, if you're not confident enough to showcase your abilities, no one will recognize or reward you. Without confidence, even the most talented individuals struggle to reach their full potential. But with confidence, the sky becomes just the starting point.

That was the experience of Mickel, a teenage boy in high school. Mickel was smart but was always too scared to speak up in class. He often had ideas, but the thought of sharing them made his heart race like an airplane preparing for takeoff. One day, his teacher, Mr. Jackson, noticed Mickel's struggle and decided to talk to him about it. This led to a short conversation between Mickel and his teacher:

"Mickel," he said, *"I know you're intelligent. Why don't you speak up in class?"* Mickel mumbled, *"I just find it really hard, sir. I wish I could be more confident and speak up, not just in class, but everywhere."*

"Don't be afraid to share your ideas. From now on, I want you to challenge yourself to raise your hand at least once in every class. Start small. Maybe just ask a question. Then work your way up to answering questions and sharing your thoughts." Those were Mr. Jackson's words to Mickel.

Though nothing seemed to change immediately, that conversation became the beginning of something significant in Mickel's life. Mr. Jackson didn't quite realize how much impact his words would have on Mickel in the coming days and later in life.

At last, Mickel decided to give it a try. The first time he raised his hand, his voice shook a little, and he felt like everyone was staring at him. But he did it. And you know what? It wasn't as bad as he thought it would be. Soon, his classmates began to notice how smart he was, and teachers praised him for his contributions each time.

As Mickel grew more confident, he joined the debate team and sought opportunities to showcase himself. He was initially nervous, but each time he remembered his teacher's encouraging words, he felt inspired to continue.

Due to his excellent performance, his team won their first competition. Mickel suddenly realized how good he was at public speaking. Soon, his newfound confidence spilled over into other areas. Later, Mickel started helping his classmates with tough subjects and made new friends. He even ran for class president and won!

By senior year, Mickel was at the top of his class. He represented his school in academic competitions and led several clubs. After graduation, he got into a great college and went on to become a very successful entrepreneur.

Self-confidence makes a difference in life. Mickel's story clearly shows how much of a difference self-confidence can make in the life of every young teenage boy who is willing to build it. Amazingly, it all started with a little push from his high school teacher.

1. Self-Confidence Is The Key To Unlocking Your Greatness

When you understand the importance of confidence, it will motivate you to pay the price to become self-confident. Here are a few powerful reasons why you should cultivate self-confidence:

2. It Increases Your Risk Quotient

When you are confident, your risk quotient increases significantly. The risk quotient refers to your ability to take risks. It means you are willing to take on projects that literally scare you. When a person is truly confident, they can take huge risks that lead to outstanding results. A confident person is willing to try things out, regardless of the odds. They are mentally prepared to face the consequences of their actions. And even when they fail, they quickly rise again, knowing they have taken the right steps.

3. It Boosts Your Performance

Confidence greatly impacts the quality of your performance, whether it's in academics, sports, or public presentation. Now, imagine for a moment that you are about to take a major test, participate in a school tournament, or compete in a debate. You might feel nervous and wonder how you'll perform.

That is where confidence becomes relevant. When you believe in yourself, something powerful stirs within you. It's as if your brain gets an extra boost of power, allowing you to maintain focus, think more clearly, and perform at your best. This is not merely an assumption. Reliable research shows that confident people do better in school, sports, and various other activities.

For example, a student with confidence will raise their hand to ask or answer questions in class. That kind of confidence directly leads to better grades in school and greater success in life. The impact of confidence doesn't stop there; it affects every part of your life.

For instance, confident athletes are known to perform better under pressure in sports. The reason comes down to something we discussed earlier in the previous chapter: They're not afraid to take risks. Because of that, they can take the chance on a winning shot or try a new move. Another significant aspect of confident athletes is that they are more likely to bounce back faster from mistakes, which is crucial in any sport. This also applies to other areas like playing an instrument, giving a speech, or working on a group project. Confidence helps you shine and stand out. A Confident person steps up, embrace challenges, and constantly pushes themselves to improve.

4. Confidence Helps Build Better Relationships

Relationship is an essential factor for success in life. It's often said that your relationships can make or break you. In other words, the people you choose to surround yourself with will have a major impact on how your life will turn out in the near future. Relationships are something that requires intentional effort and decision-making; they aren't formed by chance.

Whether you are just trying to make new friends, dealing with family, or even starting to think about dating, confidence plays a huge role in how you connect with people. When you're confident, you become a social magnet. People are naturally drawn to those who are comfortable with themselves. On the other hand, when you are confident, you can start conversations that will eventually lead to long-lasting relationships, whether in school, at home, or work.

CHASE YOUR DREAMS

The more confident you are, the better your chances of pursuing your passion and chasing your dreams. Have you ever had a big dream or a seemingly odd idea but were too scared to go for it? Maybe you wanted to start a YouTube channel, go live on Facebook, learn a new skill, or join the school basketball team, but instead of moving forward with your dream, you withdrew under the intimidating voice of fear and anxiety. At that moment, all you needed was to silence that negative voice in your head and take the first step towards your dream. The exciting thing is that when you take steps that contradict the voice of fear, fear will instantly bow to the voice of your dream.

POSITION YOURSELF
FOR FUTURE SUCCESS

While the future may be uncertain, one thing is clear: confidence is a powerful foundation for success. You may not know exactly what life holds after high school or in the years ahead, but with confidence, you're better equipped to handle what comes.

Confidence is like a master key that can open doors to opportunities you might not even know exist yet. It will open doors for you in places you least expect and with the least likely people. One common trait among successful people is their willingness to step outside their comfort zone and engage in activities that drive success. Confidence helps you take uncommon steps that lead to outstanding success in life.

There are several other reasons why confidence is crucial for every teenage boy, but for this book, I have chosen to discuss the ones mentioned above. If you find other reasons, feel free to use them to inspire yourself to cultivate your self-confidence deliberately.

Here's the exciting part: confidence doesn't just apply to your life as a teenager. The confidence you build now will set you up for greater success in college, your future career, and any challenges life may present. It's not a matter of whether you will face challenges, it's whether you'll be ready when they come. That's why it's so important to understand how crucial it is to build strong confidence. And more than just understanding it, you must take action to cultivate it.

The time to start is now!

Every day of your life, you have opportunities to practice and grow your confidence, whether it's speaking up in class, trying out for a team, or being kind to yourself. These small acts of confidence usually add up over time. Remember that building confidence is a process, and it is okay if you don't feel super-confident all the time. Most successful people experience moments of self-doubt. But if you keep at it, pretty soon, it will be apparent to everyone that you are confident, and your life of success will speak for itself.

KNOW WHO YOU ARE

---◇◇---

3

CHAPTER THREE
KNOW WHO YOU ARE

"Knowledge of your identity instills a sense of confidence in you".

Knowing who you are is a difference-maker when it comes to building self-confidence. A strong sense of your identity instills confidence within you. You have to understand that behavior is controlled by identity, and adequate knowledge of yourself will give you the advantage of being sure of yourself. This clarity of self gives you an edge over those who lack self-awareness. Many teenage boys struggle with confidence because they don't fully know themselves. They're unsure of who they are or what they stand for.

Self-awareness is about knowing yourself, which

includes recognizing your strengths, weaknesses, values, and purpose. When you truly understand these qualities about yourself, you unlock a level of confidence that is unshakable. For instance, Prince William, the Prince of Wales, does not struggle with confidence. You will never see him looking unsure of himself. Of course not! He carries himself with unwavering assurance because he knows exactly who he is and understands the role he plays in the world. This understanding shapes his behavior and actions.

I'm not suggesting that you need to be a prince to be confident. However, you must know who you are to be truly confident. Think of it like a lion in the wild. The lion may not be the biggest animal out there, but it carries itself with an attitude that gives it an edge over other, larger creatures. The lion's self-awareness greatly impacts how it perceives itself, and that, in turn, affects its attitude and behavior. Because of this, it tends to dominate other animals.

If you don't know who you are, not only will situations intimidate you, but the presence of others will make you uneasy. As mentioned in the first chapter, this connection between self-awareness and confidence is crucial, and it deserves further attention. Understanding yourself is a key factor in building true confidence.

You Are Unique in Every Way.

Understanding and embracing your uniqueness is a key step in building your self-confidence. The most important thing you must recognize about yourself is that you are truly one-of-a-kind. In other words, there has never been, and will never be, another person exactly like you. I am talking about who you are: a combination of talents, experiences, personality traits, and potential. If you take the time to reflect on this, it will immediately boost your confidence. Think about it: You are fearfully and wonderfully created, that makes you special. Amazingly, this level of uniqueness was not an accident; it was originally intended and crafted by God, your Creator. Here are a few things that make you unique. Some of them are internal, while others are external.

1. Your DNA

The first internal factor that defines your uniqueness, not only as a teenage boy but more so as a human being, is your DNA. Your DNA forms your unique genetic code, which you inherit at conception, and which is unlike anyone else's. This is the most foundational level of uniqueness. DNA influences everything from your physical traits, like eye color, to certain aspects of your personality. Even identical twins, who share nearly the same genes, have slight variations that make each person distinct.

2. Your Experiences

The second thing that defines your uniqueness is your experiences. Every single moment of your life contributes to making you who you are. Yes, someone else may have a similar experience, but no matter how similar it may seem, it will always be a different blend of circumstances than yours. And that makes you unique. Think about every conversation, every lesson learned, every triumph, and sometimes the setbacks you experience in your life, each one plays a role in shaping you. In other words, no one can truly say they have lived your life.

3. Your Talents And Skills

Another powerful factor that sets you apart is your unique combination of talents, gifts, and skills. You might have a natural ability with numbers, making math come easily for you, a skill not everyone has. It could also mean you excel in music and art or have developed impressive cooking skills. You may be great at sports or have the ability to make people laugh. Your specific blend of talents and skills is yours alone, and that makes you stand out.

4. Your Personality

Your personality traits add another layer to what makes you unique. The way you think, feel and behave is distinctly you. Some people are naturally more outgoing, while others are reserved. Whether you're an introvert or an extrovert, analytical or creative, your personality traits combine to form a one-of-a-kind profile that sets you apart.

5. Your Perspective

Your perspective on the way you see the world is also unique to you. Your experiences and thoughts shape how you view life, and that worldview guides how you live. This personal lens through which you interpret life can provide insights that no one else can offer.

KNOW YOUR IDENTITY IN CHRIST

Now, if you're a Christian, your identity goes even deeper. As a Christian, you share in the identity of Christ, which goes beyond human characteristics alone, So, this chapter isn't only about understanding yourself as a unique individual but also about knowing who you are in Christ. The Bible shares some incredible truths about our identity as Christians:

1. You Are A Child Of God

John 1:12 says, *"Yet to all who did receive him, to those who believed in his name, he gave the right to become children of God. Reflect on that for a moment: the Creator of the universe calls you, His child! What does it mean to be a child of God? It means you have a Father who loves you unconditionally, is always there for you, and has your best interests at heart. Just like a loving parent wants the best for their child, God wants the best for you. Practical application: Next time you feel alone or unsure, remind yourself, "I am a child of God. The Creator of the universe is my Father, and He loves me."*

2. You Are Chosen

As a Christian, you are chosen by God to be part of His family. While you made the personal choice to accept Christ into your heart as your Lord and Savior, before you were born, God saw you and chose you in Him. The Bible puts it this way: *"For he chose us in him before the creation of the world to be holy and blameless in his sight."* (Ephesians 1:4). Before the world even existed. I know this may be difficult for you to understand, but that means you're not an accident or an afterthought. God specifically chose you to be part of His family. And that was responsible for some circumstances leading to your salvation. He didn't choose you because you were perfect but to make you holy and blameless.

3. You Are A New Creation

When you accept Christ into your heart, a powerful transformation takes place in your spirit—you become a new creation in Him.

"Therefore, if anyone is in Christ, the new creation has come: The old has gone, the new is here!" (2 Corinthians 5:17). This new identity doesn't mean all your challenges vanish instantly. Rather, it means that you receive a fresh start spiritually. Now, your past no longer defines who you are; instead, it's your new nature in Christ that shapes you going forward.

4. You Are Royalty

One of the most mind-blowing truths about your new life in Christ is that you are royalty. The Bible tells us that we are a chosen generation and a royal priesthood: *"But you are a chosen people, a royal priesthood, a holy nation, God's special possession."* (1 Peter 2:9). As a believer, you are not just a regular person; you are special.

In ancient times, priests were considered special because they had direct access to God. Do you know what it meant to have access to God in those days? It meant a lot. Today, because of Christ, every believer has this direct access. Back then, priests served as intermediaries, bridging the gap between God and people. When the Bible calls you part of a "royal priesthood," it's acknowledging your noble standing and the significance of your relationship with God. Now, tell me, how much better can it get? That is a powerful confidence booster!

GOD LOVES YOU UNCONDITIONALLY

God's reason for sending His Son to die on the Cross was His boundless love for humanity. The book of Romans assures us that nothing can separate us from God's love (Romans 8:3). As great as that is, it is even more powerful to realize that if you were the only sinner on earth, who needed saving Christ would have died for you. That is amazing!

YOU HAVE A UNIQUE PURPOSE

In Christ, you have a specific and unique purpose that God designed for you before you were born. That purpose is one of the greatest sources of confidence. Ephesians says, *"...we are God's handiwork, created in Christ Jesus to do good works, which God prepared in advance for us to do."* (Ephesians 2:10)

Understanding your identity in Christ goes beyond feeling good about yourself; it's about knowing the truth of who God says you are. When you genuinely grasp such truths, it radically changes how you see yourself and how you approach life. These truths are more than words to inspire you—they are divine promises meant to be meditated on and embraced fully. When you take the time to reflect on and believe these truths, confidence becomes an inevitable result. However, knowing who you are is just the beginning.

Living out your God-given identity takes courage. It's a bold step to embrace who God has called you to be and to walk in that purpose daily. I challenge you to discover your unique self in Christ and find the strength to live out that identity. Always remember this powerful truth: You are more than you think.

STRIVE FOR COMPETENCE IN EVERYTHING YOU DO

4

CHAPTER FOUR
STRIVE FOR COMPETENCE IN EVERYTHING YOU DO

"When you know your stuff, confidence becomes almost automatic".

Have you ever watched a great soccer player effortlessly maneuver the ball, skillfully dribbling past opponents on the pitch? Or seen a professional basketball player showcase flawless command of the ball? Watching someone excel at what they do can be mesmerizing. They make it look so easy and magical that it might inspire you to jump onto the pitch alongside them. But before you act, remember nothing is as simple as it seems. The secret behind that apparent ease can be summed up in one word: Competence. Competence is your gateway to unshakable confidence, your true superpower.

Take Cristiano Ronaldo, for example, one of the greatest soccer players of all time.

One thing Cristiano Ronaldo is famous for is his extraordinary free kicks. When he steps up to take one, he stands still, feet planted, eyes locked on the goal. He takes a deep breath, and then boom! The ball arcs gracefully over the wall of defenders and curves perfectly into the top corner of the net. It looks effortless, almost magical. You might think, how easy! But the truth is, it's anything but easy. Achieving such precision is nearly impossible for most, but Ronaldo makes it look simple because of one key factor: Practice.

Ronaldo didn't become a free-kick master overnight. He's spent countless hours on the training ground perfecting his technique, taking thousands of free kicks to learn precisely how to position his body, strike the ball, and create that signature curve. Each free kick he takes during a game is backed by an immense amount of preparation and repetition. His confidence comes from knowing he's done it successfully so many times before. In essence, practice is the secret. The more skilled and prepared you are, the more confident you'll feel. Competence, in simple terms, means you know what you're doing in a particular area of life. It's about being skilled, knowledgeable, and prepared. When you master your craft and truly know your stuff, confidence becomes almost automatic.

What happens when you ask Roger Bannister to run a 100-meter dash, Michael Jordan to sink free throws? Do you imagine they'll start fidgeting, nervous and unsure? Of course not. Why? Because they excel at what they do. Their competence gives them the confidence to perform effortlessly, leaving you marveling at their expertise and perhaps questioning your skills. What's the takeaway? It's simple: Competence fuels confidence.

Competence and confidence are like inseparable best friends—one strengthens the other. Think about it. When you truly know your stuff, whether it's solving algebra problems, shooting hoops, or playing the guitar, you naturally feel more assured and ready to perform. That's the competence-confidence connection (CCC) at work. The better you get at something, the more confident you become in it.

BATTLING FEAR AND ANXIETY

Many times, fear and anxiety reveal ignorance and a lack of thorough preparation. While it's true that even well-prepared people can feel nervous, much of the anxiety we experience comes from doubts about our readiness. Could it be that your nerves are telling you to study more, practice harder, or prepare better? Yes, almost everyone experiences those "butterflies" before a big presentation or performance. But here's the thing: when you've done the work, when you've studied, practiced, and prepared thoroughly those butterflies can quickly transform into confidence. So, the next time you feel nervous about something, ask yourself: "Have I done everything I can to prepare?" You may feel those butterflies, but as soon as you break the ice and switch into competence mode, it silences fear and replaces it with self-assurance. The anxiety butterflies will suddenly give way to the flight of confidence. Fear fades when preparation shines.

CONFIDENCE IS TASK-SPECIFIC

Confidence is not a one-size-fits-all trait; it is task-specific. This means that the confidence you display in one area may not automatically translate to another. For example, someone who excels in public speaking may feel completely out of their depth when operating a computer or playing video games. Similarly, you might dominate at video games but feel unsure when it comes to addressing a crowd. And that's perfectly normal! The reason is quite simple: You've spent much time playing video games, practicing and improving. But if you've never really done much public speaking, of course, you'll feel less sure of yourself, leading to a lack of confidence in that area. If you've never had much exposure or practice in something, you're bound to feel less confident.

This is why people tend to avoid tasks or roles they feel unprepared for they lack the skills, knowledge, or practice that would otherwise make them feel capable. Confidence builds through familiarity and mastery, so the key to growing it in any area is to actively work on developing your abilities there. It's all about practice and preparation!

PRACTICE MAKES CONFIDENCE

Imagine a young boy who has spent hours practicing his free throws in basketball. When he steps onto the court to compete, his confidence is naturally higher because he's practiced and honed his skills. On the other hand, an angry kid who is just stepping onto the court for the first time may feel uncertain, because his knowledge and experience are limited. This is the power of confidence that comes from practice.

PREPARE LIKE DAVID AND JOSEPH

You've probably heard the saying, "Practice makes perfect," but I have a better one for you: "Preparation makes confidence." When you're well-prepared for something, it feels like you're wearing armor against any challenge. There are powerful examples of the power of preparation in the Bible, not only in the story of Esther but also in the lives of David and Joseph.

1. **David's Preparation**

David's story is a remarkable one when it comes to preparation. As a young shepherd, he faced wild animals like lions and bears and learned to defend his flock. But his true test of preparation came when he faced the giant, Goliath. While the entire army of Israel was paralyzed with fear, David was ready. Why? Because he had spent years preparing, not in military tactics or training for hand-to-hand combat, but in trusting God in every battle he faced.

When the opportunity came to face Goliath, David knew he could defeat the giant because he was spiritually prepared. He had been practicing his faith, his courage, and his trust in God's power. With nothing but a slingshot and stones, David stepped onto the battlefield with confidence because of his preparation, and as we know, he defeated Goliath. David's preparation was not about the size of his army or weapons; it was about the strength of his trust in God.

2. Joseph's Preparation

Similarly, Joseph's preparation was both long and challenging, yet it led to his destiny. Joseph was sold into slavery, falsely accused, and imprisoned, yet during these years of hardship, he was being prepared for leadership. Every trial Joseph faced was a lesson in humility, perseverance, and trusting God's plan, even when circumstances seemed hopeless.

When the time came for Joseph to interpret Pharaoh's dream and rise to the position of second-in-command in Egypt, he did so with confidence because of his years of preparation through adversity. His experiences in the pit, the prison, and the palace all prepared him for the responsibility he would later bear. His confidence wasn't in his own ability but in the faithfulness of God and the lessons he had learned in his journey.

THE PRINCIPLE OF PREPARATION

Just like Esther, David, and Joseph, the more you prepare, the more confident you will feel when the moment arrives. Esther spent a year preparing to meet the king, David spent years learning to trust God in the fields, and Joseph spent years in hardship, preparing for leadership. They didn't just rely on talent or external circumstances; they relied on their inner preparation, which equipped them for their God-given purpose. The principle is simple: the more you prepare, the more confident you'll be. Confidence doesn't come from mere hope or wishful thinking; it comes from being ready. Whether it's through hard work, personal growth, or spiritual training, when you prepare well, you walk into your challenge with the armor of confidence, knowing you are ready to face whatever comes your way.

So, like David and Joseph, take time to prepare for your destiny. Prepare your heart, mind, and spirit. And when the moment comes, you will walk into it with the same confidence they had because preparation makes confidence.

DISCOVER AND DEVELOP
YOUR POTENTIAL

To truly become competent, you must first discover and then develop your potential, gifts, and talents. Each one of us has been uniquely gifted with skills and abilities that make us who we are. But these talents, if left undiscovered or undeveloped, remain untapped and may not amount to much. Imagine, for a moment, that you are holding a seed in your hand.

This seed holds the potential to grow into a magnificent, strong tree. But if you simply leave it sitting on your desk, nothing will happen. To see it thrive, you need to plant it in fertile soil, water it, and ensure it receives the sunlight it needs. With time and care, it will begin to grow, eventually becoming a towering tree that provides shade, beauty, and benefits to all who come near.

In the same way, you are like that seed. You have incredible potential within you, but to make the most of it, you must take the necessary steps to nurture it. You need to discover what you are truly good at, what excites you, and what you feel passionate about. Once you've found those things, you must dedicate time and effort to practice, learn, and grow in those areas until you reach mastery. This won't happen overnight, but with patience and persistence, you will eventually become all that you were created to be.

One of the ways to do this is to start trying out new things. Trying new activities and stepping out of your comfort zone allows you to explore hidden talents you might not have realized you possess. Whether it's art, music, public speaking, or problem-solving, exploring new things pushes your limits and expands your abilities. As you discover areas where you have a natural flair, you can deepen your knowledge and skills. The more you practice and develop, the more competent and confident you will become. Remember, growth takes time. Be patient with yourself as you discover and develop your potential. Keep watering the seed of your talent, and watch it grow into something extraordinary.

PUSH TO LEARN FAST

My advice to you is simple but powerful: master the ability to learn quickly. When you can learn fast, you unlock the ability to develop any skill you need for success. In today's rapidly changing world, the ability to adapt and learn quickly is one of your most valuable assets. It doesn't just help you perform better in school (although that's certainly a plus), but it also positions you for better opportunities beyond the classroom.

Being a quick learner means you can adjust to new environments and situations with ease. Whether it's a new job, a new project, or a shift in technology, your ability to adapt quickly makes you more confident in facing these challenges. This confidence, powered by competence, allows you to navigate the world more effectively.

Keep in mind, that becoming truly great at what you do is not about achieving perfection. It's about continual learning and growth. It's about-facing challenges head-on, learning from your mistakes, and consistently striving to improve. As you focus on developing your skills, your competence will naturally increase, which in turn boosts your confidence. This confidence will enable you to take on bigger challenges, creating a cycle of growth, success, and achievement in your life. By pushing yourself to learn quickly and continuously, you set yourself up for a future where your competence and confidence work together to open doors to new opportunities. So, start sharpening your learning skills today you'll thank yourself tomorrow.

EMBRACE
A GROWTH
MINDSET

5

CHAPTER FIVE
EMBRACE A GROWTH MINDSET

"When growth kicks in, confidence builds up."

If you want to be a confident teenager who grows into a confident adult, embracing a growth mindset is essential. As a teenage boy, you're at a pivotal stage in life where your personal growth can have a significant impact on your future. At every stage of life, you are either making progress or going backward, depending on your decision to adopt a growth mindset. A growth mindset not only influences your growth but also directly impacts your confidence. But before we dive into how it shapes your confidence, let's first understand what a growth mindset is all about.

The term "growth mindset" was first used by psychologist Carol Dweck, and this idea has dramatically changed how we think about learning, intelligence, and personal growth. But what exactly is a growth mindset, and why is it so crucial for teenage boys? Here are some popular definitions that might be helpful:

A growth mindset is the belief that your abilities, intelligence, and talents can be developed through effort, learning, and persistence. Someone with a growth mindset believes, "This is where I am now, and this is what I am good at, but if I focus on growth, I can become better and capable of more." It's a mindset that's rooted in the idea that effort leads to improvement and that setbacks are learning opportunities.

But here's the catch: embracing a growth mindset requires you to be willing to face discomfort and challenges. Growth often happens outside of your comfort zone, and you need to put yourself in situations that encourage you to push beyond your limits. This means that to build the confidence that comes with a growth mindset, you must be prepared to face challenges head-on. Many young people want to grow, but they shy away from challenges because they don't like feeling uncomfortable. However, true growth only occurs when you're willing to take on challenges.

The opposite of a growth mindset is a fixed mindset. A fixed mindset is the belief that your intelligence, talents, and skills are static that you either have them or you don't, and nothing can change that. Someone with a fixed mindset might say, "This is who I am, this is what I know, and this is all I'll ever be capable of." They avoid challenges because they fear failure, believing it reflects their inherent limitations.

Sadly, many young people feel this way, which is why they struggle when faced with the challenges that life presents. However, if you choose to embrace a growth mindset, you'll unlock your full potential, increase your confidence, and be ready to take on whatever comes your way.

Always remember this: confidence comes from knowing that you can grow, adapt, and improve. So, adopt a growth mindset, embrace challenges, and watch your confidence soar.

YOU NEED A GROWTH MINDSET

As a teenage boy, adopting a growth mindset can truly transform your life. The teenage years are filled with challenges puberty, peer pressure, self-esteem issues, academic stress, and the many other hurdles of growing up. On top of that, the world around you is changing rapidly, presenting even more challenges. To thrive through all of these, it's crucial that you keep growing, learning, and improving. This is where a growth mindset becomes essential.

A growth mindset allows you to approach challenges differently. Instead of seeing obstacles as threats or reasons to give up, you begin to view them as opportunities to learn and grow. This mindset shift empowers you to face difficulties head-on and turn setbacks into valuable lessons.

In every area of your life, whether it's school, sports, or personal relationships, a growth mindset will help you keep moving forward. It helps you see potential where others might see failure, and it gives you the resilience to keep going even when things get tough. By adopting a growth mindset, you're not just preparing to face the challenges of today you're equipping yourself for a lifetime of success and confidence. It's not about being perfect or having everything figured out. It's about being willing to grow, learn from mistakes, and embrace new opportunities. With a growth mindset, you can unlock your true potential and overcome any challenges that come your way.

GROWTH MINDSET AND CONFIDENCE

Now that we understand the concept of a growth mindset, let's explore how it directly affects your confidence. A growth mindset prepares you to face difficult tasks, rather than shy away from them. Instead of seeing challenges as barriers, you begin to see them as opportunities to learn and grow. This mindset shift is crucial because every time you face a challenge and overcome it; you prove to yourself that you are capable. Each victory, no matter how small, boosts your self-belief and strengthens your confidence.

One of the biggest confidence killers for teenage boys is the fear of failure. Many young people associate failure with a reflection of their worth, believing that if they fail, it means they are not good enough. However, with a growth mindset, you can separate your failures from your identity. You begin to view failure not as a measure of your worth but as an essential part of learning. This shift allows you to protect and maintain your confidence, even when things don't go as planned.

When you understand that failure is a natural part of the growth process, you are more likely to take risks and step outside your comfort zone. It's this willingness to try new things, despite the fear of failing, that helps you grow and, in turn, builds your confidence.

A growth mindset also teaches you that effort is the key to mastery. When you believe that you can improve through hard work and perseverance, you're more likely to put in the time and energy needed to develop new skills. The best part is, as you put in the effort, your confidence naturally grows. You start to see yourself improving in different areas of life whether it's academics, sports, or relationships, and that growth fuels your self-belief. The more you trust in your ability to learn and adapt, the more confident you become.

Ultimately, a growth mindset doesn't just help you become better at what you do, it builds your confidence in your ability to overcome obstacles and achieve success, no matter what challenges you face.

"For our light affliction, which is but for a moment, worketh for us a far more exceeding and eternal weight of glory; while we look not at the things which are seen, but at the things which are not seen: for the things which are seen are temporal; but the things which are not seen are eternal." 1 Corinthians 4:18

First, it says they are light afflictions, meaning they are not as severe as you might think. This suggests that God sees your challenges from a different perspective than you do. His interpretation of what you are going through is entirely different from yours. Secondly, it states that they are for a moment. Yes, it may have lasted a whole school year, but God says it is for a moment. It may have caused you many sleepless nights, but God says it's just a moment. Again, this means that how God sees these challenges is different from how you see them.

Another crucial aspect of that scripture is that it says the things seen (which include whatever challenges you are facing right now) are temporal. The word *"temporary"* can be translated as "subject to change." You must realize that every challenge you face is subject to change. Have you encountered a setback lately and are wondering how to recover? Or have you failed an exam or fumbled at a competition? I want you to understand that they are all subject to change and do not define your worth. The key is in your response to those challenges.

That brings us to the importance of resilience. Resilience is the ability to recover from setbacks, adapt to change, and keep going despite challenges. Every time you bounce back from a setback, your confidence grows. Why? Because resilience teaches you that failure is not permanent; it's simply a steppingstone on the path to success. Each time you face a difficulty head-on and overcome it, you gain strength, knowledge, and a deeper confidence in your ability to rise above any challenge.

In essence, resilience builds confidence. It helps you trust in your ability to navigate the storms of life and emerge stronger. When you embrace setbacks as opportunities to grow, you develop the mental toughness and determination that breed self-assurance. As you face difficulties with resilience, you reinforce the belief that no matter what comes your way, you are equipped to handle it. Your challenges will pass, and you will come out stronger, on the other side more confident and capable.

THE GROWTH MINDSET

A growth mindset doesn't just impact your actions, it also transforms the way you talk to yourself. Your inner dialogue, the ongoing conversation you have with yourself, plays a significant role in shaping your confidence. With a growth mindset, you shift from harsh self-criticism to positive self-talk, encouraging and motivating yourself to face challenges head-on.

Think about it this way, when you make a mistake or fall short of a goal, do you say things like, "I'm such a failure," or do you say, "I made a mistake, but I can learn from this and do better next time"? A person with a growth mindset leans toward the second option. They recognize that setbacks are not permanent and that every misstep is an opportunity to grow and improve.

There are a few things you must learn to develop a growth mindset. Let's look at some of them:

1. Learn To Use The Word "Yet":

When you say you can't do things, you paralyze yourself and rob yourself of the opportunity to try. But when you learn to use the word "yet," you are taking the limits off and letting your inner self know that whatever you can't do now is only temporary.

No matter how difficult something may be, the moment you add the word "yet," you open up the opportunity for growth and improvement. What that little word does for you is acknowledge that though you are not there yet, you are willing to go through the process to improve. That way, you are developing a growth mindset.

2. Celebrate The Process:

You will have to pass many hurdles before you achieve the results you are trying to accomplish. Those are parts of the process. Don't just focus all your energy on the results; learn to enjoy the process. If you understand this, you will focus on more than just the grade in school but on studying and preparing for it. Your priority will become ensuring you've given your best effort to achieve the results you desire rather than simply focusing on the outcome. Celebrate your courage during the process. By valuing the process of growth and learning, you will be more motivated to keep pushing yourself, regardless of immediate outcomes.

3. Set Goals For Learning New Things:

You can either set goals on what to achieve or gain new knowledge and skills. Setting learning goals has a powerful impact on our growth mindset. While setting goals for better grades is important, it is even better to set goals focused on personal growth and skill development. Keep in mind that success starts with being before it evolves into doing or having. That's what you do when you decide to personally understand the law of thermodynamics, osmosis, or any topic or concept in any subject you study in school. You could also work on improving how you communicate and connect with your classmates. These types of goals encourage you to focus more on the learning process rather than just the result, therefore, helping you develop a growth mindset.

4. Think About Your Learning:

After you have learned something new to improve yourself or your skills, take time to reflect on it. That is how you make it a part of you. One way you can do that is to keep a journal. In your journal, write down new things you are learning and, perhaps, challenges you are currently dealing with. When you do that, you'll start to notice your progress and reinforce the understanding that you are continually growing and improving.

5. See Your Mistakes As Opportunities To Learn:

Growth and mistakes go hand-in-hand. If you want to develop a growth mindset you must embrace the confidence to make them. Mistakes are okay in fact, if you're not making any, it only means one thing: you are not trying anything new or challenging yourself. Just like someone who never writes on a board avoids getting their hands dirty, avoiding mistakes limits your ability to create meaningful outcomes. But it's in trying out things that you create the outcomes you want. Don't allow the fear of mistakes to rob you of the opportunity to unlock and unleash your potential. Instead, see mistakes as learning opportunities. Even when you make mistakes, take them in good faith, learn from them, and move on to other things. Consider better ways of doing the same things and keep trying until you see improvement. By treating mistakes as valuable lessons rather than failures, you'll be more likely to persist in overcoming challenges.

6. Seek out challenges:

Don't run from challenges; face them! When you run from challenges, you run from opportunities. Instead, intentionally put yourself in situations that stretch your abilities. That could mean taking on a harder class, trying a new sport, or volunteering for a leadership role in a club. Remember, it's through challenges that we grow the most. Otherwise, you will remain in one spot for a long time.

As you embrace the culture of growth, understand that nothing happens overnight but over time. Your confidence will develop slowly. You will have to keep at it. By cultivating a growth mindset and committing to the keys I have just provided for you, you'll develop greater self-assurance and unlock your full potential. Your teenage years are a powerful period for self-discovery and transformation. By embracing these principles and practices, you're building confidence for today and laying the foundation for a fulfilling and successful future.

SELF-CONFIDENCE HABITS

CHAPTER SIX
SELF-CONFIDENCE HABITS

"If you can do certain things every day, they will boost your confidence in life."

Habits are powerful factors in shaping our lives. If you want to succeed, you must develop good habits. It's often said that you don't decide your future; you decide your habits, and your habits decide your future. The secrets of a person's life lie in their daily routine. Success, growth, and great accomplishments stem from cultivating the right habits

When it comes to self-confidence, there are specific habits you can cultivate that will help transform your belief in yourself. Self-confidence isn't just a feeling it's something you build over time through consistent action. To boost your confidence, you need to take deliberate actions regularly. Making these actions part of your routine is the foundation for strong self-confidence.

Think of it like physical strength. If you want to get stronger, you'll need to commit to exercising consistently, not just occasionally. It's the same with confidence: simply admiring someone else's confidence won't do; you need to take action and stay consistent to build your own. Just like building muscles takes regular effort, so does building the muscles of your self-belief. Consistency is key.

Just like with physical fitness, building confidence requires consistent effort. By practicing certain habits daily, you are training your mind to be more confident, much like you would train your muscles to become stronger. This chapter is about developing those habits that will enhance your self-confidence. However, a word of caution: these habits aren't quick fixes or magical solutions. They are practical, actionable steps you can take each day to gradually boost your confidence. At first, they may feel strange or difficult, but remember, all new habits come with challenges. With time and practice, these habits will become second nature, and your confidence will grow steadily.

Habit #1: Setting And Achieving Small Goals

One of the most powerful ways to boost your self-confidence is by setting and achieving small, manageable goals. Accomplishing what you set out to do proves to yourself that you are capable, which directly impacts the way you view your abilities. This is the foundation of confidence in keeping promises to yourself, not just to others. When you say you'll do something and follow through, it strengthens your self-belief.

Often, when we think of goals, we focus on big achievements like getting straight A's or speaking at a big event. However, smaller goals like waking up early or going to bed on time are just as important. They may seem simple but accomplishing them brings a sense of fulfillment and sets the stage for bigger successes.

Big goals can feel overwhelming, and that's why breaking them down into smaller, more manageable steps is essential. Smaller goals are easier to track and complete and accomplishing them boosts your morale and confidence. For instance, if your goal is to improve your grades, instead of simply saying, "I want an A," break it down into smaller goals: study for 20 minutes after school, ask at least one question in class each week, or review your notes for 10 minutes before bed. These small, specific tasks are achievable and allow you to see progress more clearly. Achieving each small goal not only brings you closer to your larger objective but also strengthens your belief in your ability to succeed, which significantly boosts your confidence.

Habit 2: Positive Self-Talk And Affirmations

Positive self-talk on the other hand serves as your inner cheerleader, reminding you of your potential and progress. Instead of tearing yourself down, you learn to uplift and encourage yourself. This practice not only helps you build resilience but also maintains and reinforces your confidence.

For example, when faced with a difficult task, someone with a fixed mindset might think, "I can't do this; I'm just not good at it." But with a growth mindset, the thought would shift to, "This is tough, but with effort and practice, I'll improve." These positive affirmations, although simple, are incredibly powerful in fostering confidence in your abilities. When you become your own biggest supporter, your confidence flourishes. You no longer rely solely on external validation to feel good about yourself.

Instead, you trust the strength of your inner voice, which tells you, "I am capable, and I can overcome this." Embracing this mindset not only nurtures your confidence but also sets you up for lasting success and fulfillment in all areas of life.

Self-talk refers to the internal dialogue we have with ourselves, and what we say to and about ourselves significantly impacts our confidence. You have the power to choose whether your self-talk is positive or negative, and amazingly, it's entirely up to you.

For many, especially during the teenage years, that inner voice can be quite critical. It may tell you that you're not good enough or that you'll mess things up. If you let these negative thoughts dominate, they can erode your confidence. However, the great news is that you can change this voice from negative to positive.

You need to consciously speak to yourself in ways that uplift and encourage you. Think of it as being your own best friend or personal cheerleader. Instead of saying things like, "I can't do this," or "I'm so stupid," replace them with affirmations such as, "I can overcome this challenge," or "I'm still learning, and that's okay." By acknowledging the difficulty of a situation without letting it define you, you declare your resilience and ability to push through. This shift in self-talk will help boost your confidence and overall mindset.

When you say positive things about yourself, it significantly impacts your confidence. Positive self-talk isn't about ignoring challenges or pretending everything is perfect. It's about approaching challenges with an "I can do it" attitude. It's about recognizing the difficulty while also reminding yourself of your ability to handle it.

Affirmations are a powerful tool for positive self-talk. Here are a few positive statements you can repeat regularly to reassure yourself and boost your confidence. Learn to tell yourself:

- *"I am capable of handling whatever comes my way."*
- *"I am constantly growing and improving."*
- *"I have unique talents and strengths to offer the world."*
- *"I can do all things through Christ who strengthens me."*
- *"Greater is He that is in me than he that is in the world."*

Habit 3: Taking Care Of Your Physical Health

There is a strong connection between your physical health and your confidence, even though many people may not realize it. Taking care of your health is not only about achieving fitness or looking good, but it also plays a significant role in boosting your confidence. Your physical health directly influences how you perceive yourself and your self-esteem. Each time you invest in your health, you are affirming your worth. Recognizing your value is key to improving yourself. When you feel physically strong and healthy, you are more likely to have the energy and positive mindset to face challenges, which in turn enhances your confidence.

To maintain a healthy body, focus on the right diet, regular exercise, and sufficient sleep. As a teenager, your body and brain are still developing, so sleep is crucial for recharging your energy. Eating well doesn't mean following a strict diet; it's about fueling your body with the right nutrients. Include a variety of fruits, vegetables, whole grains, and lean proteins in your meals. Make sure to never skip meals, especially breakfast, as your brain needs fuel to stay sharp throughout the day.

Hydration is also key. Aim for 6-8 glasses of water

daily. If you find plain water boring, you can infuse it with fruit for natural flavor. And don't forget about personal hygiene. Taking care of your appearance and cleanliness is another important factor that contributes to how you feel about yourself.

Habit 4: Stepping Out Of Your Comfort Zone

To build your confidence, you need to learn how to step out of your comfort zone. The comfort zone provides a sense of security, safety, and control. But when you step outside of it, you enter a space of uncertainty and discomfort, where you may feel like you're losing control. This can be intimidating. However, it's only by stepping out of your comfort zone that you can achieve great things in life. Every time you take on a challenge or do something that makes you nervous, you expand your comfort zone. You prove to yourself that you can handle more than you thought, and that is where true confidence grows. Make stepping out of your comfort zone a daily habit, and you'll cultivate a powerful, uncommon confidence.

Habit 5: Practicing Gratitude

Gratitude is a powerful confidence booster. It's not about doing more or being more, but about appreciating what you already have and who you are. Practicing gratitude shifts your focus from what you lack to what you have, which creates a positive mindset that can greatly enhance your confidence. When you take time to recognize the good things in your life, you acknowledge your worth, the people who support you, and the challenges you've overcome. This helps build a stronger sense of self and a deeper confidence. Gratitude allows you to appreciate the skills you've gained, the progress you've made, and the value of your experiences.

Many more self-confidence habits can help you grow, such as surrounding yourself with supportive people, continually learning, helping others, and giving back. For this book, I've highlighted a few key habits. I encourage you to embrace and practice them consistently. By doing so, you'll experience lasting changes in how you see yourself and ultimately boost your confidence.

DEVELOP GOD CONFIDENCE

―――∽∼∿◇◇∿∼∽―――

7

CHAPTER SEVEN
DEVELOP GOD CONFIDENCE

"When you are sure that God is right behind you, your confidence goes through the roof."

Your confidence in God is a cornerstone of true self-confidence. When you encounter someone brimming with confidence, especially a believer, there's often an unshakable awareness that their strength comes from something far greater than themselves. This becomes particularly evident when they accomplish things that surpass their natural abilities, relying not on their power but on what God can do through them.

One of the biggest secrets to self-confidence is awareness of your connection to God. You cannot be aware that God is with you and for you and still surrender to fear. There is such a thing as God-confidence, or, put another way, confidence in God. Another word for that is faith. Faith is a force that compels the cooperation of the Almighty God to work on your behalf.

I know that we have talked about several other secrets to confidence, but if we fail to discuss the subject of faith, a major piece of the puzzle will be missing. When you come to your wits' end, when you come to the end of your confidence in your abilities, competence, and all of the wonderful things we have discussed, you need to know that you can fall back on something more powerful than fear, anxiety, or challenges themselves. I am talking about God Almighty himself.

While we've explored various pathways to building confidence, the role of faith is indispensable. It fills the gaps when your own abilities or resources fall short. Faith provides an anchor in moments of uncertainty and a source of courage to overcome fear and anxiety. When you cultivate confidence in God, you're not just leaning on your strength but drawing from an infinite well of divine power. With this foundation, you're equipped to face life's challenges with resilience and unwavering assurance.

Faith is a product of revelation from God, resulting in absolute confidence in God and His word. When God speaks to you, faith is born in your heart. Once faith is born in your heart, the challenges you face or the crowd before you won't matter anymore. You will stand tall, knowing God is right there with you. I mean, if God is for you and with you, what force can make you unsure or doubtful?

The proof that you have faith is the corresponding action. When faith is present, action flows naturally. When you hear God's voice, that voice will inspire you to take corresponding action, regardless of how awkward you may feel about the situation. Yes, there is a place of knowing or conviction, as we clearly see in the book of Mark:

"For verily I say unto you, That whosoever shall say unto this mountain, Be thou removed, and be thou cast into the sea; and shall not doubt in his heart, but shall believe that those things which he saith shall come to pass; he shall have whatsoever he saith. Therefore, I say unto you, What things soever ye desire, when ye pray, believe that ye receive them, and ye shall have them." Mark 11:23-24

If you truly believe or are convinced of something, you must declare it boldly and courageously. However, belief alone isn't enough to achieve your desires, it must be followed by action. How does this apply to you? For instance, if you believe you will succeed in life, that belief should drive you to take the necessary steps, such as preparing adequately for it.

In essence, confidence in God inspires the right actions, and those actions, in turn, strengthen your feelings of confidence. The amazing thing about this process is that one step inspires another. Taking action leads to results, which then encourage you to take even more action, producing greater outcomes. This cycle of belief, action, and results reinforces itself, creating momentum for continued success. Although this concept has been discussed earlier, it is worth emphasizing again here.

DAVID AND GOLIATH

When we cultivate confidence in God, it becomes the foundation for overcoming challenges in every other area of life. This principle is powerfully demonstrated in the Bible through the story of David. His victory over Goliath illustrates how one triumph, fueled by faith, can lead to many more.

Goliath was huge beyond imagination. He was a literal giant born into a family of giants. Later in scripture, we see that he had other brothers (2

Samuel 21:18). Goliath was not only a physical giant but also a well-trained soldier. In other words, David was nothing compared to Goliath, both in size and weaponry. Goliath was huge and strong. The Bible reveals that he was over nine feet tall!

David was just a young shepherd, while Goliath was a towering, well-trained warrior who struck fear into the entire Israelite army. Goliath wasn't just an imposing figure he was a literal giant from a family of giants, as the Bible later indicates in (2 Samuel 21:18). His size, strength, and weaponry were unmatched. Standing over nine feet tall, Goliath wore a bronze helmet, a 125-pound coat of armor, bronze leg protection, and carried a spear with a 15-pound iron tip. In addition, he was a walking tank, a seemingly invincible foe.

Despite being significantly outmatched, David, a mere teenager, dared to step forward when even seasoned soldiers were paralyzed by fear. His boldness wasn't rooted in physical strength or experience but in his unshakable confidence in God. At just 17 years old, David dared to confront the formidable Goliath when no one else would. This act of faith and courage stands as a testament to what can happen when you place your trust in God.

David had God-confidence.

David's confidence was truly rooted in his faith in God rather than his own abilities. He wasn't simply an ordinary boy taking a random shot at greatness; he had a strong, proven relationship with God that shaped his confidence. While David was skilled with a slingshot, a tool commonly used by the Benjamites, it wasn't his skill alone that guaranteed victory. After all, a slingshot against a nine-foot-tall, heavily armored warrior like Goliath seemed like an impossible match. David's assurance came from the God who had been faithful to him time and time again.

In 1 Samuel 17:36, we learn that David had already faced life-threatening challenges before stepping onto the battlefield with Goliath. He had single-handedly killed both a lion and a bear to protect his father's sheep. These experiences not only showcased his bravery but also reinforced his confidence in God's ability to deliver him.

This teaches us an essential lesson: overcoming smaller challenges builds the confidence and faith needed to face larger ones. Every time you step out of your comfort zone whether it's solving a problem, learning something new, or standing up in class you're strengthening yourself for the bigger battles ahead.

David's story is about more than defeating a giant; it's about the courage to confront what seems impossible because of a deep trust in God. When Goliath cursed David in the name of his gods, David didn't shrink back. He boldly declared victory in the name of the Lord and then ran toward Goliath with fearless determination.

David's confidence was indeed the epitome of *"small boy, big God."* It reminds us that no matter how daunting the challenge, confidence in God gives us the courage to face it head-on.

"Then said David to the Philistine, Thou comest to me with a sword, and with a spear, and with a shield: but I come to thee in the name of the LORD of hosts, the God of the armies of Israel, whom thou hast defied. This day will the LORD deliver thee into mine hand, and I will smite thee, and take thine head from thee, and I will give the carcasses of the host of the Philistines this day unto the fowls of the air, and to the wild beasts of the earth; that all the earth may know that there is a God in Israel. And it came to pass, when the Philistine arose, and came and drew nigh to meet David, that David hasted, and ran toward the army to meet the Philistine." 1 Samuel 17:45-46, 47.

David's triumph over Goliath serves as a powerful reminder that victory comes not from human strength, strategy, or resources but from placing unwavering trust in God. Though David's slingshot seemed insignificant compared to Goliath's massive size and advanced weaponry, it became a tool for divine intervention.

When Goliath fell, David didn't hesitate; he seized the moment, using Goliath's own sword to complete the victory. In 1 Samuel 17:50, David prevailed without a sword in his hand a testament to the fact that his victory was rooted in God's power, not human might.

This story shows that when we have confidence in God, no challenge, no matter how intimidating, can overwhelm us. God doesn't need us to have the perfect tools or flawless skills. He simply needs us to trust Him and act in faith. When you learn to rely on God in every challenge, you gain a boldness that transforms fear into faith. With God on your side, your victory is not just possible it's assured. Whatever "giants" you face in life, know that confidence in God will empower you to overcome them and emerge victorious!

LIVE THE FEARLESS LIFE

CHAPTER EIGHT
LIVE THE FEARLESS LIFE

"When you learn to overcome fear, you are ready to walk in absolute confidence."

Fear and self-doubt are among the greatest obstacles to building true confidence. To embark on the journey toward confidence, it is essential to learn how to overcome these internal barriers. While eliminating fear and self-doubt might seem impossible, you can rise above them, leading a life of boldness and self-assurance. This chapter is dedicated to equipping you with practical techniques and strategies to help you do just that. Whenever fear or uncertainty creeps in, recognize it for what it is an obstacle that can be conquered. A fearless life doesn't mean never feeling fear or doubt; it means not allowing them to control you. It's about cultivating such a strong foundation of confidence that nothing intimidates you enough to hold you back. By mastering these strategies, you can move closer to becoming the person you were meant to be, unshaken by the challenges and doubts that arise.

TWO OF A KIND

Fear and self-doubt often work hand in hand, like twins. While their roles are distinct, they are so closely related that it's hard to talk about one without the other. Fear whispers, "Something bad might happen. "In many ways, fear is like an overprotective parent. It's not inherently bad it's your brain's way of protecting you from potential harm. For example, when your parents were nervous about your first bike ride or your first time skiing, it wasn't because they didn't want you to learn and grow. They simply wanted to ensure your safety. Similarly, fear can be helpful when it steers you away from real dangers. But much like an overprotective parent, fear can sometimes overstep, keeping you from taking risks that lead to growth and exciting new opportunities.

Self-doubt, on the other hand, is the voice that says, *"Are you sure you're capable?"* or "You're not good enough." It often comes from past failures, unfavorable comparisons to others, or persistent negative self-talk. Unlike fear, which warns of external risks, self-doubt attacks your internal sense of capability, undermining your confidence and limiting your potential.

Together, these two forces fear, and self-doubt can create a powerful barrier that holds you back from trying new things, stepping out of your comfort zone, or realizing your full potential. Recognizing how they work is the first step toward overcoming them and moving forward with courage and self-belief.

FEAR AND SELF-DOUBT: DESIGNED TO PARALYZE YOU

Fear and self-doubt share a common goal: to paralyze you and stop you from acting. Their mission is to keep you from stepping out, taking calculated risks, or pursuing opportunities that could change your life. But here's a truth you must embrace everything worthwhile in life comes with some level of risk. Those who are bold enough to take risks are the ones who enjoy the rewards that come with them. The relationship between risk and reward is simple: the greater the risk, the greater the potential reward. Unfortunately, fear can make you hesitate, filling your mind with "what ifs," while self-doubt makes you question whether you're even capable of succeeding. Together, these feelings can be so overwhelming that they paralyze you, keeping you stuck in place. Have you ever experienced that moment when fear took over, and you felt like you couldn't move? That's how powerful and debilitating fear can be. It freezes you, convincing you that taking any step forward is too risky or that you're not good enough to succeed. But here's the thing: just because fear and self-doubt are common doesn't mean they should control you.

You must either conquer fear, or it will conquer you. If left unchecked, these two forces will block you from achieving your goals and becoming all, you are capable of being. The good news is that they can be overcome, and you can learn to live fearlessly with total confidence.

Now, let's explore a few simple yet powerful strategies to break free from their grip and step boldly into your future.

1. Focus On Building Your Confidence

Fear has a sneaky way of stealing the spotlight. It magnifies what could go wrong, turning potential opportunities into imagined disasters. Even if you're fully capable, fear plants seeds of doubt, making you question your abilities. Fear can paralyze you, affect your body language, and chip away at your confidence. The key is not to fight fear directly but to shift your focus toward building confidence. Fear thrives when it has your attention. The more you focus on it, the stronger it becomes. But the moment you turn your attention to cultivating confidence, fear begins to lose its grip. Confidence grows with focus and practice, and as it grows, it naturally diminishes fear. Remember, what you give your energy to is what flourishes. If you dwell on fear, it will overpower you. But when you actively work on your confidence whether by practicing, preparing, or stepping out of your comfort zone it becomes the dominant force in your life. Choose to focus on your confidence, and watch fear take a backseat.

2. Learn To Stand Up For Yourself

Part of living a fearless life is learning to stand up for yourself. That doesn't mean being aggressive or mean to people. It means valuing yourself enough to assert your needs and boundaries. It begins with knowing your worth. I don't want to stress this too much because I've already written a full chapter on knowing who you are. But here is the point: You need to know your worth to be truly confident and fearless. Standing up for yourself requires practice in saying "no." A lot of young people think there is something wrong with saying no, and that is how they get themselves into various troubles.

It's okay to turn down requests that don't align with your values or priorities. When someone invites you to a party that you know won't benefit you or will distract you from your studies, you must say, "No." You don't need to be rude, but you must be firm enough in your convictions to say "no" without feeling guilty.

Now, here is what I want you to do at least give it a try: Think of something you often agree to even though you don't want to. From now on, when it comes up, boldly say "no." When you begin to act this way and take control of your choices, your confidence level will start to increase significantly.

3. Learn To Set Boundaries

Setting boundaries is an essential part of building confidence. It means deciding what you're comfortable with and communicating that to others. If something bothers you, don't keep it bottled up inside speak up. Your feelings and opinions are important, and if you don't express them, no one else will. For example, if a friend repeatedly makes jokes at your expense, it's okay to politely but firmly let them know their comments hurt and ask them to stop. Confidence gives you the strength to identify what you will and won't accept and empowers you to address issues directly and respectfully. Remember, boundaries are about protecting your well-being, not about being confrontational. Setting them up is a sign of self-respect and confidence in your worth.

4. Discover God's Word On Fear

The second secret to overcoming fear is to understand and embrace God's word on fear. The fear you feel is not from God. When you realize that, you will take a stand against it and overcome it. When you know it's not from God, then you know that God can empower you above it. Furthermore, realize that fear is not just a feeling but a spirit (an evil spirit). For those who are believers, we know that God has not given us such a spirit. *"For God has not given us a spirit of fear, but of power and love and a sound mind."* 2 Timothy 1:7 (NKJV)

God has given you and me much better power, love, and a sound mind. In other words, fear is just an impostor. You need to understand these three elements that God has given you to take full advantage of them.

First, there's power, and power does not just refer to

physical strength but to the ability to face challenges, persevere, and stand firm in your beliefs. The second is love, which begins with love for God and love for other people. When you operate in love, there's no room for fear. The Bible says that perfect love casts out fear (1 John 4:18). Then, of course, there is the sound mind we receive as believers. A sound mind goes beyond intelligence; it is mainly about having self-control, discipline, and clear thinking. A person who has a sound mind cannot be confused or panicked.

5. Follow The Examples Of Daniel

There are several biblical examples of those who chose to live a fearless life. I have already talked about David in the previous chapter. But then, there is the case of Daniel. Daniel was a young Jewish man living in Babylon who was taken captive in a land far from his homeland. However, despite being in a foreign culture, Daniel stood firm in his beliefs. At one time, some people plotted to eliminate him based on his faith in God and his commitment to a life of prayer.

A law was even passed to stop Daniel from praying to God for 30 days. But Daniel continued to pray to God as he always did. He knew this could get him into big trouble, but he was confident in his faith in God. He was practically fearless! The result was that he was thrown into a den of lions.

As we see in the story, God secured Daniel's life from the lions. Daniel's story teaches us that true confidence isn't always about feeling safe or comfortable.

You are going to face many dangers that will confront you at times, but you must choose to be fearless, knowing that God has your back. If you choose to practice the principles we have discussed in this chapter, you will position yourself to live a fearless life. The choice is completely yours!

MENTORSHIP AND CONFIDENCE: THE ROLE OF ROLE MODELS

9

CHAPTER NINE
MENTORSHIP AND CONFIDENCE: THE ROLE OF ROLE MODELS

HOW SEEKING GUIDANCE FROM MENTORS CAN HELP BUILD CONFIDENCE

Mentorship is one of the most powerful tools for boosting confidence, particularly for young people navigating their personal and academic journeys. A mentor is someone with experience, wisdom, and insight who can offer guidance, advice, and encouragement. By seeking mentorship, you tap into a wealth of knowledge that can help you make better decisions, avoid common mistakes, and gain the confidence needed to face challenges head-on.

Having a mentor can help you:

1. Gain Perspective And Clarity.

Mentors offer an outside perspective that helps you see your strengths and weaknesses objectively. They can help you clarify your goals and break them down into achievable steps, which can reduce anxiety and build confidence in your ability to succeed.

2. Learn From Their Experiences.

A mentor has likely faced challenges similar to yours and can share valuable lessons learned. This can help you avoid repeating your mistakes and give you the confidence to try new things, knowing that failure is just a steppingstone to growth.

3. Build Accountability.

A mentor keeps you accountable, providing gentle encouragement when you need it and holding you to your commitments. This accountability fosters discipline and determination, which are essential for building confidence in your abilities and accomplishments.

4. Develop Emotional Support.

Mentors provide emotional support when you face setbacks, reminding you that it's okay to struggle and encouraging you to keep pushing forward. Their unwavering belief in your potential can have a lasting impact on your confidence.

THE IMPORTANCE OF SURROUNDING YOURSELF WITH PEOPLE WHO ENCOURAGE AND UPLIFT YOU

In addition to mentors, the people you surround yourself with play a significant role in shaping your confidence. It's essential to build a support system of friends, family, or community members who uplift you and believe in your abilities. When you're surrounded by positive influences, you are more likely to believe in yourself and take risks that lead to growth.

Here's why surrounding yourself with encouraging people is crucial

1. Positive Reinforcement

Being around people who genuinely care about your success helps you stay motivated. They celebrate your achievements and encourage you when you're feeling down. This constant positive reinforcement strengthens your self-belief and makes it easier to stay confident in your abilities.

2. Emotional Safety

Confidence grows when you feel safe to be yourself. Surrounding yourself with people who respect and accept you creates an environment where you can take risks without the fear of judgment. Emotional safety allows you to make mistakes, learn, and grow, without feeling like a failure.

3. Increased Resilience

Life is filled with obstacles, but when you have a strong support system, you're less likely to give up when things get tough. Encouraging people help you see challenges as opportunities for growth, not as roadblocks. Their belief in you strengthens your resilience, which directly impacts your confidence.

4. Constructive Criticism

True friends and mentors don't just tell you what you want to hear—they also offer constructive feedback that helps you improve. Surrounding yourself with people who give you honest, respectful feedback allows you to learn from your mistakes and build the skills you need to grow. This process helps you develop confidence in your ability to improve and succeed.

5. Empathy And Understanding

When people understand your struggles and provide empathy, it validates your feelings and experiences. Knowing you're not alone in your challenges boosts confidence because you realize that setbacks are part of everyone's journey. This sense of shared experience strengthens your resolve to keep moving forward.

HOW TO FIND MENTORS AND BUILD A SUPPORTIVE CIRCLE

To fully benefit from mentorship and the power of uplifting people, take proactive steps to find the right mentors and surround yourself with positive influences:

1. **Seek Out Mentors:** Look for people who have qualities or experiences you admire. This could be teachers, coaches, family members, or professionals in your field of interest. Don't hesitate to reach out and ask for advice or guidance.

2. **Engage in Communities:** Join clubs, sports teams, or online groups where people share similar interests. These communities often foster relationships built on mutual support and encouragement.

3. **Be Open to Feedback:** Encourage honest feedback from your mentor and peers. Accepting constructive criticism with an open mind helps you grow and shows that you're committed to improving.

4. **Practice Gratitude:** Express appreciation for the people who uplift and encourage you. Gratitude strengthens relationships and reinforces the positive impact these individuals have on your confidence.

Mentorship and surrounding yourself with people who believe in you are vital to building lasting confidence. By seeking guidance, learning from others' experiences, and fostering relationships that encourage growth, you can boost your self-esteem and take on challenges with greater self-assurance. Remember, confidence is not built in isolation it flourishes when nurtured by a community of supporters who believe in your potential.

DAILY PRAYER FOR TEEN BOY

Dear God,

Thank you for the gift of life and for creating me in the image of your beloved Son, Jesus Christ. I am grateful for your everlasting mercy and your grace that is always sufficient. Thank you for the wonderful people you've placed in my life; bless my parents, family, teachers, and friends. Please guide me in making wise decisions today and lead me in everything I do. Give me the courage to face any challenges ahead. Fill me with divine wisdom, knowledge, and understanding, and help me to be a positive example to my friends. May my efforts in class be crowned with good success. Please protect me and keep me from harm. Guard my heart, mind, eyes, and ears from the evil in this world, and let your angels watch over me. As I go out today, may the words I speak and the thoughts I think bring you honor and be pleasing to you. In Jesus' name, I pray. Amen.

DAILY DECLARATIONS

1. I am a child of God

John 1:12: But to all who did receive him, who believed in his name, he gave the right to become children of God.

2. I shall not die but live

Psalm 118:17 - I shall not die, but live, and declare the works of the Lord.

3. I am the light of the world

Matthew 5:14 - You are the light of the world. A city set on a hill cannot be hidden.

4. I have the life of Christ in me

Galatians 2:20 - I have been crucified with Christ. It is no longer I who live, but Christ lives in me.

5. I am led by the Spirit of God

Romans 8:14 - For all who are led by the Spirit of God are sons of God.

6. I am protected by the blood of Jesus

Revelation 12:11 - And they overcame him by the blood of the Lamb and by the word of their testimony.

7. I am safe from harm and danger

Psalm 91:11 - For He will command His angels concerning you to guard you in all your ways.

8. I am a wonder to my generation

Psalm 71:7 - I have become a wonder to many, but you are my strong refuge.

9. I am fearfully and wonderfully made

Psalm 139:14 - I praise you, for I am fearfully and wonderfully made. Wonderful are your works; my soul knows it very well.

10. I am blessed and highly favored by God

Luke 1:28 - And he came to her and said, 'Greetings, O favored one, the Lord is with you.

11. No weapon formed against me shall prosper

Isaiah 54:17 - No weapon that is fashioned against you shall succeed, and you shall refute every tongue that rises against you in judgment.

10. I know that all things work together for my good

Romans 8:28 - And we know that in all things God works for the good of those who love him, who have been called according to his purpose.

11. I can do all things through Christ who strengthens me

Philippians 4:13 - I can do all things through Christ who strengthens me.

12. With God on my side I will not be afraid of anything

Psalm 118:6 - The Lord is on my side; I will not fear. What can man do to me?

13. I am confident in God, because in Him I move, I live, and have my being

Acts 17:28 - For in him we live and move and have our being.

14. I am a chosen generation

1 Peter 2:9 - But you are a chosen generation, a royal priesthood, a holy nation, His own special people, that you may proclaim the praises of Him who called you out of darkness into His marvelous light.

15. I am a standard bearer of the Kingdom

Isaiah 62:10 - Go through, go through the gates! Prepare the way for the people; build up, build up the highway! Remove the stones, lift up a banner for the people.

www.ingramcontent.com/pod-product-compliance
Lightning Source LLC
Chambersburg PA
CBHW070643050426
42451CB00008B/285